My Divorce Journal

Divorce (also known as the dissolution of marriage) is the process of ending a legal marriage. The laws regarding this process varies considerably in each country or state but customarily, divorce requires the sanction of a court or such other authority in a legal process. Additionally, depending on the circumstances it may involve issues relating to the determination and distribution of matrimonial assets, children arrangements (including financial provisions, visitation and education), spousal support and even restraint orders.

KEY TIPS

Things to consider during this process

- ### IS YOUR MARRIAGE REALLY OVER? BEFORE YOU START DIVORCE PROCEEDINGS MAKE SURE THE ANSWER IS YES.

First, do not file divorce proceedings only to send a message to your partner. You may have threatened to get divorced in the past and your partner would say they do not want to lose you. However, once you actually take steps to get divorced, everything changes. Before you do that, make absolutely sure it is what you want to do. The process can be costly and even if public funding provided, it may be limited, so make sure it is truly over before you take the leap. Ask yourself, is marriage counseling an option? Is mediation and option? Maybe legal separation an option? Educate and put yourself in the best position by having a consultation with an experienced divorce attorney.

- ### MONITOR YOUR FEELINGS, TALK TO A PROFESSIONAL IF NECESSARY AND DECLARE POSITIVE AFFIRMATIONS FOR YOUR LIFE

It is not always easy, so give yourself permission to let go and if you need someone who you can talk to in confidence, seek a therapist or counselor. You will need someone who can listen and help you give objective advice or coaching on the various emotions you will be feelings and ways to cope.

- ### SET YOUR GOALS AND MAKE A PLAN

The wedding took some planning and so will the separation/ divorce. You have to take this seriously and plan. This will save you costs, stress and disappointment at the end. You have to put in the time and dedication in to achieve what you want and make a plan for how to get it. While it does mot guarantee you will get everything you want at least you will have a plan and be able to communicate that effective to your estranged spouse, lawyer or the court

- ### GET GOOD LEGAL ADVICE FROM AN EXPERIENCED DIVORCE ATTORNEY

We all have friends who went through a separation or divorce but they are not the person you should be taking advice from initially. Having a simple consultation with an Attorney can assist you with the direction, issues regarding children and assets, timeline and costs. Then you can choose to sign a retainer agreement or not but you need legal advice.
You may have to pay for a consultation otherwise find a Legal Befriendsers clinic or Legal Aid Clinic that provide free advice. Please avoid handling your divorce yourself, without getting appropriate legal advice / representation, particularly if the other side is represented. Your employer, bank or lending institution may provide loans for legal proceedings.
Make sure to create a list of questions for your lawyer during the consultation. Some questions should include:
- Retainer amount for divorce proceedings and the payment arrangements for refresher payments
- The number of years' experience that Attorney has with family law
- The Attorney's current workload capacity to handle your matter and how many other paralegals or junior Attorneys will be billing on this matter.
- Confirming that conflict checks have been completed
- Whether they accept legal aid or if you even may qualify for legal aid

KEY TIPS (CONTINUED)

Things to consider during this process

- ### RETAIN COPIES OF ALL YOUR EXPENSES, FINANCIAL DOCUMENTS AND ASSETS IN A SAFE PLACE

ff your divorce is cordial, you may be able to get your financial papers any time. But, when a divorce gets unpleasant, financial documents tend to go missing. Since it is impossible to know in advance whether your divorce will go smoothly (even if you want it to do so) the wisest thing you can do is to get copies of all of the financial documents you will need for your divorce as soon as possible and store in a safe place. You will also need to calculate your monthly needs and provide a budget to your Attorney and the Court if financial orders are being requested.

if you were married in another State of country, you may have to obtain the registered copy of the marriage certificater to file. Also keep copies of your children's birth certificate and any other important document needed to assist your case.

- ### SERIOUSLY CONSIDER PROFESSIONAL MEDIATION

lYour divorce Attorney charges an hourly rate. They are not your friend and they are billing you for everything! All communications, court appearance, reports and researched is logged and billed to you. The divorce process is not necessarily a quick one and the court system can take an extended time securing hearing dates. If you can communicate with your estranged spouse and narrow some of the issues that would assist greatly. You don't have to agree with everything that offer. But the more you can talk to your e-partner and hammer out your own agreement, the quicker, cheaper, and easier your divorce will be.

- ### THE INTEREST OF THE CHILDREN ARE PARAMOUNT

A court must have regard to the best interests of the child as the paramount consideration in any family proceedings.
The court is aware parents sometimes uses children as bargaining chips in divorce proceedings or settlement matters. It is important to understand that contested children proceedings can be costly and draining and not in the child's best interest.
A few things the court looks at are:
- The emotional ties and relationships between parents
- The capacity of the parents to provide a safe home and adequate food, clothing, and medical care
- The mental and physical health needs of the child
- The mental and physical health of the parents
- The presence of domestic violence in the home
- The child's wishes (depending on their age and understanding)

KEY TIPS (CONTINUED)
Things to consider during this process

- ### EDUCATE YOURSELF BUT DO NOT DO IT YOURSELF

There is a great deal of information online and everyone knows someone who went through a divorce, but your experience is unique. And while some divorces are simply and not contentious, the likelihood of mistakes increases (and costs) when you doing the filing of documents on your own. Take the time to research your concerns and discuss it with a professional. That professional should always make time for you (with reasonable notice provided) and should make you feel safe to discuss all issues. Listen to your Attorney and if necessary get a second opinion from another Attorney. This is why keeping a journal is important.

- ### TAKE RESPONSIBILITY, KEEP DETAIL NOTES AND PARTICIPATE IN ALL MATTERS THAT CONCERNS YOUR DIVORCE

This is your life, your divorce and only you can provide the insight into your needs and priorities. While it may be tempting to ignore that email or call and just binge watch Netflix or crawl in bed that will not assist your position. You are having a bad day, write that down. Having a good day, write that down and celebrate it. Then get up and start all over again, review your notes and refocus. Do not be a passive party to your own divorce - take control. However, make reasonable and rational decisions after getting the necessary advice from your professional. This will save you tons of money.

SELF-LOVE & AFFIRMATION

List of things to appreciate
during this process

DATE: Grateful For

List of Affirmations

_____

_____

_____

_____

My Achievements

○ _____   ○ _____

○ _____   ○ _____

○ _____   ○ _____

○ _____   ○ _____

Motivational Quote

_____

_____

_____

SELF-LOVE & AFFIRMATION

List of things to appreciate
during this process

DATE: **Grateful For**

List of Affirmations

My Achievements

- ○ _____
- ○ _____
- ○ _____
- ○ _____

- ○ _____
- ○ _____
- ○ _____
- ○ _____

Motivational Quote

SELF-LOVE & AFFIRMATION

List of things to appreciate
during this process

DATE: **Grateful For**

List of Affirmations

My Achievements

- ○ _____
- ○ _____
- ○ _____
- ○ _____

- ○ _____
- ○ _____
- ○ _____
- ○ _____

Motivational Quote

SELF-LOVE & AFFIRMATION

List of things to appreciate
during this process

DATE: Grateful For

List of Affirmations

My Achievements

- ○ _____
- ○ _____
- ○ _____
- ○ _____

- ○ _____
- ○ _____
- ○ _____
- ○ _____

Motivational Quote

SELF-LOVE & AFFIRMATION

List of things to appreciate
during this process

DATE: Grateful For

List of Affirmations

_____

_____

_____

_____

_____

My Achievements

○ _____ ○ _____

○ _____ ○ _____

○ _____ ○ _____

○ ○

Motivational Quote

_____

_____

_____

SELF-LOVE & AFFIRMATION

List of things to appreciate
during this process

DATE: Grateful For

List of Affirmations

_____
_____
_____
_____

My Achievements

○ _____   ○ _____
○ _____   ○ _____
○ _____   ○ _____
○   ○

Motivational Quote

_____
_____

SELF-LOVE & AFFIRMATION

List of things to appreciate
during this process

DATE: **Grateful For**

List of Affirmations

My Achievements

- ◯ _____
- ◯ _____
- ◯ _____
- ◯ _____

- ◯ _____
- ◯ _____
- ◯ _____
- ◯ _____

Motivational Quote

SELF-LOVE & AFFIRMATION

List of things to appreciate
during this process

DATE: Grateful For

List of Affirmations

My Achievements

○ _____

○ _____

○ _____

○ _____

○ _____

○ _____

○ _____

○ _____

Motivational Quote

SELF-LOVE & AFFIRMATION

List of things to appreciate
during this process

DATE: Grateful For

List of Affirmations

My Achievements

○ _____
○ _____
○ _____
○ _____

○ _____
○ _____
○ _____
○ _____

Motivational Quote

SELF-LOVE & AFFIRMATION

List of things to appreciate
during this process

DATE: Grateful For

List of Affirmations

_____

_____

_____

_____

My Achievements

- ○ _____
- ○ _____
- ○ _____
- ○ _____

- ○ _____
- ○ _____
- ○ _____
- ○ _____

Motivational Quote

_____

_____

_____

MY PRIORITIES

DATE:

_____

_____

_____

_____

MY PRIORITIES

DATE:

_____

_____

_____

_____

MY PRIORITIES

DATE:

_____

_____

_____

_____

MY PRIORITIES

DATE:

_____

_____

_____

_____

"THE FIRST STEP TO SUCCESS IS KNOWING YOUR PRIORITIES." ASPESH

MY PRIORITIES

DATE:

NOTES FOR ATTORNEY

DATE:

_____

_____

_____

_____

_____

_____

_____

_____

_____

_____

_____

_____

_____

_____

_____

_____

_____

_____

_____

DON'T BE AFRAID. BE FOCUSED. BE DETERMINED. BE
HOPEFUL. BE EMPOWERED." – MICHELLE OBAMA

NOTES FOR ATTORNEY

DATE:

_____

_____

_____

_____

_____

_____

_____

_____

_____

_____

_____

_____

_____

_____

_____

_____

_____

_____

_____

_____

_____

DON'T BE AFRAID. BE FOCUSED. BE DETERMINED. BE
HOPEFUL. BE EMPOWERED." – MICHELLE OBAMA

NOTES FOR ATTORNEY

DATE:

_____

_____

_____

_____

_____

_____

_____

_____

_____

_____

_____

_____

_____

_____

_____

_____

_____

_____

_____

DON'T BE AFRAID. BE FOCUSED. BE DETERMINED. BE
HOPEFUL. BE EMPOWERED." – MICHELLE OBAMA

NOTES FOR ATTORNEY

DATE:

_____

_____

_____

_____

_____

_____

_____

_____

_____

_____

_____

_____

_____

_____

_____

_____

_____

_____

DON'T BE AFRAID. BE FOCUSED. BE DETERMINED. BE
HOPEFUL. BE EMPOWERED." – MICHELLE OBAMA

NOTES FOR ATTORNEY

DATE:

_____

_____

_____

_____

_____

_____

_____

_____

_____

_____

_____

_____

_____

_____

_____

_____

_____

_____

DON'T BE AFRAID. BE FOCUSED. BE DETERMINED. BE
HOPEFUL. BE EMPOWERED." – MICHELLE OBAMA

NOTES FOR
ATTORNEY

DATE:

_____

_____

_____

_____

_____

_____

_____

_____

_____

_____

_____

_____

_____

_____

_____

_____

_____

_____

DON'T BE AFRAID. BE FOCUSED. BE DETERMINED. BE
HOPEFUL. BE EMPOWERED." – MICHELLE OBAMA

NOTES FOR ATTORNEY

DATE:

_____

_____

_____

_____

_____

_____

_____

_____

_____

_____

_____

_____

_____

_____

_____

_____

_____

DON'T BE AFRAID. BE FOCUSED. BE DETERMINED. BE
HOPEFUL. BE EMPOWERED." – MICHELLE OBAMA

NOTES FOR ATTORNEY

DATE:

_____

_____

_____

_____

_____

_____

_____

_____

_____

_____

_____

_____

_____

_____

_____

_____

_____

_____

_____

DON'T BE AFRAID. BE FOCUSED. BE DETERMINED. BE
HOPEFUL. BE EMPOWERED." – MICHELLE OBAMA

NOTES FOR ATTORNEY

DATE:

_____

_____

_____

_____

_____

_____

_____

_____

_____

_____

_____

_____

_____

_____

_____

_____

_____

_____

_____

DON'T BE AFRAID. BE FOCUSED. BE DETERMINED. BE
HOPEFUL. BE EMPOWERED." – MICHELLE OBAMA

NOTES FOR ATTORNEY

DATE:

_____

_____

_____

_____

_____

_____

_____

_____

_____

_____

_____

_____

_____

_____

_____

_____

_____

_____

_____

DON'T BE AFRAID. BE FOCUSED. BE DETERMINED. BE
HOPEFUL. BE EMPOWERED." – MICHELLE OBAMA

NOTES FOR ATTORNEY

DATE:

_____

_____

_____

_____

_____

_____

_____

_____

_____

_____

_____

_____

_____

_____

_____

_____

_____

DON'T BE AFRAID. BE FOCUSED. BE DETERMINED. BE
HOPEFUL. BE EMPOWERED." – MICHELLE OBAMA

NOTES FOR ATTORNEY

DATE:

_____

_____

_____

_____

_____

_____

_____

_____

_____

_____

_____

_____

_____

_____

_____

_____

_____

_____

DON'T BE AFRAID. BE FOCUSED. BE DETERMINED. BE
HOPEFUL. BE EMPOWERED." – MICHELLE OBAMA

NOTES FOR ATTORNEY

DATE:

_____

_____

_____

_____

_____

_____

_____

_____

_____

_____

_____

_____

_____

_____

_____

_____

_____

DON'T BE AFRAID. BE FOCUSED. BE DETERMINED. BE
HOPEFUL. BE EMPOWERED." – MICHELLE OBAMA

NOTES FOR ATTORNEY

DATE:

_____
_____
_____
_____
_____
_____
_____
_____
_____
_____
_____
_____
_____
_____
_____
_____
_____
_____
_____
_____
_____

DON'T BE AFRAID. BE FOCUSED. BE DETERMINED. BE
HOPEFUL. BE EMPOWERED." – MICHELLE OBAMA

NOTES FOR ATTORNEY

DATE:

_____

_____

_____

_____

_____

_____

_____

_____

_____

_____

_____

_____

_____

_____

_____

_____

_____

_____

_____

_____

DON'T BE AFRAID. BE FOCUSED. BE DETERMINED. BE
HOPEFUL. BE EMPOWERED." – MICHELLE OBAMA

NOTES FOR ATTORNEY

DATE:

_____

_____

_____

_____

_____

_____

_____

_____

_____

_____

_____

_____

_____

_____

_____

_____

_____

_____

_____

_____

DON'T BE AFRAID. BE FOCUSED. BE DETERMINED. BE HOPEFUL. BE EMPOWERED." – MICHELLE OBAMA

NOTES FOR COURT

DATE:

_____

_____

_____

_____

_____

_____

_____

_____

_____

_____

_____

_____

_____

_____

_____

_____

_____

_____

DON'T BE AFRAID. BE FOCUSED. BE DETERMINED. BE
HOPEFUL. BE EMPOWERED." – MICHELLE OBAMA

NOTES FOR COURT

DATE:

_____

_____

_____

_____

_____

_____

_____

_____

_____

_____

_____

_____

_____

_____

_____

_____

_____

_____

_____

DON'T BE AFRAID. BE FOCUSED. BE DETERMINED. BE
HOPEFUL. BE EMPOWERED." – MICHELLE OBAMA

NOTES FOR COURT

DATE:

_____

_____

_____

_____

_____

_____

_____

_____

_____

_____

_____

_____

_____

_____

_____

_____

_____

_____

DON'T BE AFRAID. BE FOCUSED. BE DETERMINED. BE
HOPEFUL. BE EMPOWERED." – MICHELLE OBAMA

NOTES FOR COURT

DATE:

_____

_____

_____

_____

_____

_____

_____

_____

_____

_____

_____

_____

_____

_____

_____

_____

_____

_____

DON'T BE AFRAID. BE FOCUSED. BE DETERMINED. BE
HOPEFUL. BE EMPOWERED." – MICHELLE OBAMA

NOTES FOR COURT

DATE:

_____

_____

_____

_____

_____

_____

_____

_____

_____

_____

_____

_____

_____

_____

_____

_____

_____

_____

DON'T BE AFRAID. BE FOCUSED. BE DETERMINED. BE
HOPEFUL. BE EMPOWERED." – MICHELLE OBAMA

NOTES FOR COURT

DATE:

_____

_____

_____

_____

_____

_____

_____

_____

_____

_____

_____

_____

_____

_____

_____

_____

_____

_____

DON'T BE AFRAID. BE FOCUSED. BE DETERMINED. BE
HOPEFUL. BE EMPOWERED." – MICHELLE OBAMA

NOTES FOR COURT

DATE:

_____

_____

_____

_____

_____

_____

_____

_____

_____

_____

_____

_____

_____

_____

_____

_____

_____

_____

DON'T BE AFRAID. BE FOCUSED. BE DETERMINED. BE
HOPEFUL. BE EMPOWERED." – MICHELLE OBAMA

NOTES FOR COURT

DATE:

_____

_____

_____

_____

_____

_____

_____

_____

_____

_____

_____

_____

_____

_____

_____

_____

_____

_____

_____

_____

_____

DON'T BE AFRAID. BE FOCUSED. BE DETERMINED. BE
HOPEFUL. BE EMPOWERED." – MICHELLE OBAMA

NOTES FOR COURT

DATE:

_____

_____

_____

_____

_____

_____

_____

_____

_____

_____

_____

_____

_____

_____

_____

_____

_____

_____

_____

DON'T BE AFRAID. BE FOCUSED. BE DETERMINED. BE
HOPEFUL. BE EMPOWERED." – MICHELLE OBAMA

NOTES FOR
COURT

DATE:

_____

_____

_____

_____

_____

_____

_____

_____

_____

_____

_____

_____

_____

_____

_____

_____

_____

_____

DON'T BE AFRAID. BE FOCUSED. BE DETERMINED. BE
HOPEFUL. BE EMPOWERED." – MICHELLE OBAMA

NOTES FOR COURT

DATE:

_____

_____

_____

_____

_____

_____

_____

_____

_____

_____

_____

_____

_____

_____

_____

_____

_____

_____

DON'T BE AFRAID. BE FOCUSED. BE DETERMINED. BE
HOPEFUL. BE EMPOWERED." – MICHELLE OBAMA

NOTES FOR COURT

DATE:

_____

_____

_____

_____

_____

_____

_____

_____

_____

_____

_____

_____

_____

_____

_____

_____

_____

_____

_____

DON'T BE AFRAID. BE FOCUSED. BE DETERMINED. BE
HOPEFUL. BE EMPOWERED." – MICHELLE OBAMA

NOTES FOR COURT

DATE:

_____

_____

_____

_____

_____

_____

_____

_____

_____

_____

_____

_____

_____

_____

_____

_____

_____

DON'T BE AFRAID. BE FOCUSED. BE DETERMINED. BE
HOPEFUL. BE EMPOWERED." – MICHELLE OBAMA

NOTES FOR COURT

DATE:

_____

_____

_____

_____

_____

_____

_____

_____

_____

_____

_____

_____

_____

_____

_____

_____

_____

_____

_____

_____

DON'T BE AFRAID. BE FOCUSED. BE DETERMINED. BE
HOPEFUL. BE EMPOWERED." – MICHELLE OBAMA

NOTES FOR COURT

DATE:

_____

_____

_____

_____

_____

_____

_____

_____

_____

_____

_____

_____

_____

_____

_____

_____

_____

DON'T BE AFRAID. BE FOCUSED. BE DETERMINED. BE
HOPEFUL. BE EMPOWERED." – MICHELLE OBAMA

PROGRESS
FOLLOW-UP

DATE:

_____

_____

PROGRESS
FOLLOW-UP

DATE:

_____

_____

PROGRESS
FOLLOW-UP

DATE:

_____

_____

PROGRESS
FOLLOW-UP

DATE:

_____

_____

PROGRESS
FOLLOW-UP

DATE:

_____

_____

PROGRESS
FOLLOW-UP

DATE:

_____

_____

PROGRESS
FOLLOW-UP

DATE:

_____

_____

TOUGH TIMES NEVER LAST BUT TOUGH PEOPLE DO."
ROBERT H. SCHULLER

PROGRESS
FOLLOW-UP

DATE:

_____

_____

PROGRESS
FOLLOW-UP

DATE:

_____

_____

PROGRESS
FOLLOW-UP

DATE:

_____

_____

MY NOTES

DATE:

MY NOTES

DATE:

TOUGH TIMES NEVER LAST BUT TOUGH PEOPLE DO."
ROBERT H. SCHULLER

MY NOTES

DATE:

_____

_____

MY NOTES

DATE:

_____

_____

MY NOTES

DATE:

_____

_____

MY NOTES

DATE:

_____

_____

MY NOTES

DATE:

_____

_____

MY NOTES

DATE:

_____

_____

MY NOTES

DATE:

_____

_____

MY NOTES

DATE:

_____

_____

MY NOTES

DATE:

_____

_____

MY NOTES

DATE:

_____

_____

MY NOTES

DATE:

_____

_____

MY NOTES

DATE:

_____

_____

MY NOTES

DATE:

_____

_____

MY NOTES

DATE:

_____

_____

MY MONTHLY BUDGET

Income		
Income-1		
Income-2		
Other Income		
	Total Income	

Expenses
Month
Budget

Bill To Be Paid	Due Date	Amount	Paid	Notes
	Total			

Monthly Summary		
Total Income	**Total Expenses**	**Difference**

Notes

MY MONTHLY BUDGET

Income			Expenses	
Income-1			Month	
Income-2				
Other Income			Budget	
	Total Income			

Bill To Be Paid	Due Date	Amount	Paid	Notes
	Total			

Monthly Summary

Total Income	Total Expenses	Difference

Notes

MY MONTHLY BUDGET

Income			Expenses	
Income-1			**Month**	
Income-2				
Other Income			**Budget**	
	Total Income			

Bill To Be Paid	Due Date	Amount	Paid	Notes
	Total			

Monthly Summary

Total Income	Total Expenses	Difference

Notes

_____
_____
_____
_____
_____
_____

MY MONTHLY BUDGET

Income		
Income-1		
Income-2		
Other Income		
	Total Income	

Expenses
Month
Budget

Bill To Be Paid	Due Date	Amount	Paid	Notes
_____	_____	_____	_____	_____
_____	_____	_____	_____	_____
_____	_____	_____	_____	_____
_____	_____	_____	_____	_____
_____	_____	_____	_____	_____
_____	_____	_____	_____	_____
_____	_____	_____	_____	_____
_____	_____	_____	_____	_____
_____	_____	_____	_____	_____
_____	_____	_____	_____	_____
_____	Total	_____	_____	_____

Monthly Summary		
Total Income	Total Expenses	Difference

Notes

_____

_____

_____

_____

_____

_____

MY MONTHLY BUDGET

Income		
Income-1		
Income-2		
Other Income		
	Total Income	

Expenses	
Month	
Budget	

Bill To Be Paid	Due Date	Amount	Paid	Notes
	Total			

Monthly Summary		
Total Income	Total Expenses	Difference

Notes

MY MONTHLY BUDGET

Income		
Income-1		
Income-2		
Other Income		
	Total Income	

Expenses
Month
Budget

Bill To Be Paid	Due Date	Amount	Paid	Notes
	Total			

Monthly Summary		
Total Income	**Total Expenses**	**Difference**

Notes

MY MONTHLY BUDGET

Income		
Income-1		
Income-2		
Other Income		
	Total Income	

Expenses
Month
Budget

Bill To Be Paid	Due Date	Amount	Paid	Notes
	Total			

Monthly Summary

Total Income	Total Expenses	Difference

Notes

_____
_____
_____
_____
_____
_____
_____

MY MONTHLY BUDGET

Income		
Income-1		
Income-2		
Other Income		
	Total Income	

Expenses	
Month	
Budget	

Bill To Be Paid	Due Date	Amount	Paid	Notes
	Total			

Monthly Summary		
Total Income	Total Expenses	Difference

Notes

MY MONTHLY BUDGET

Income		
Income-1		
Income-2		
Other Income		
	Total Income	

Expenses	
Month	
Budget	

Bill To Be Paid	Due Date	Amount	Paid	Notes
	Total			

Monthly Summary		
Total Income	Total Expenses	Difference

Notes

MY MONTHLY BUDGET

Income		
Income-1		
Income-2		
Other Income		
	Total Income	

Expenses
Month
Budget

Bill To Be Paid	Due Date	Amount	Paid	Notes
	Total			

Monthly Summary		
Total Income	Total Expenses	Difference

Notes

MY MONTHLY BUDGET

Income		
Income-1		
Income-2		
Other Income		
	Total Income	

Expenses
Month
Budget

Bill To Be Paid	Due Date	Amount	Paid	Notes
_____	_____	_____	_____	_____
_____	_____	_____	_____	_____
_____	_____	_____	_____	_____
_____	_____	_____	_____	_____
_____	_____	_____	_____	_____
_____	_____	_____	_____	_____
_____	_____	_____	_____	_____
_____	_____	_____	_____	_____
_____	_____	_____	_____	_____
	Total	_____		

Monthly Summary

Total Income	Total Expenses	Difference

Notes

_____

_____

_____

_____

_____

_____

MY MONTHLY BUDGET

Income		
Income-1		
Income-2		
Other Income		
	Total Income	

Expenses
Month
Budget

Bill To Be Paid	Due Date	Amount	Paid	Notes
	Total			

Monthly Summary		
Total Income	**Total Expenses**	**Difference**

Notes

More Notes

More Notes

More Notes

More Notes

More Notes

More Notes

More Notes

More Notes

More Notes

More Notes

More Notes